the extreme sports collection

In-Line Skating!

get aggressive

Laura Kaminker

rosen publishing group's
rosen central
new york

For Dave and Johnny

Published in 1999 by The Rosen Publishing Group, Inc.
29 East 21st Street, New York, NY 10010

First Edition

Library of Congress Cataloging-in-Publication Data

Kaminker, Laura.
    In-line skating! Get aggressive / Laura Kaminker. — 1st ed.
      p. cm. — (The extreme sports collection)
    Includes bibliographical references and index.
    Summary: Introduces the sport of aggressive in-line skating, discussing its development, equipment, basic moves, safety tips, and more.
    ISBN 0-8239-3012-2
    1. In-line skating Juvenile literature.   2. Extreme sports Juvenile literature.   [1. In-line skating.] I. Title. II. Title: In-line skating. III. Series.
  GV859.73.K36   1999
   796.21—dc21   99-22810
                                                   CIP

Manufactured in the United States of America

contents

1 What's Extreme?
4

2 What's Up with In-Line Skating?
8

3 Getting Aggressive
14

4 OUCH! Be Smart–Be Safe
19

5 You Can't Skate Without Skates
24

6 I've Got My Skates–Now What?
34

7 Getting Started–and Beyond
47

52 X-Planations
54 Extreme Info
58 Where to Play
61 Extreme Reading
62 Index
64 Credits

What's Extreme?

Let's get something straight: What is extreme to you might not be extreme to the next person. And what's extreme to that person might be tame to you. You see, "extreme" is relative. It means something different to everyone.

Not that long ago, just owning a pair of in-line skates meant you were a little bit extreme. It meant you were willing to take risks and break new ground by trying out this new

Rafael Sandor
at the 1997 X
Games, San Diego

kind of roller skate with the wheels all in a line. Then in-line skating caught on in a big way. To be extreme today, you have to add turns, jumps, and other tricks to your skating routine. You have to skate up and down ramps or stairs. You have to thrash if you want to call yourself an extreme skater.

Today there are the X Games, a sort of miniature Olympics for extreme sports. Athletes from around the world gather for this event to show just how extreme they can be. They climb ice walls, race down slippery ski slopes on mountain bikes, and jump out of airplanes with skateboards strapped to their feet. They compete to see who can grab the biggest air, hit the highest speeds, and perform the most difficult stunts. The winner for each sport is given a gold medal and the title of "Most Extreme Athlete on the Planet." Most extreme, that is, at least until the next X Games competition, when new athletes redefine what it takes to be extreme.

Jenny Curry wins the gold medal for women's street skating at the 1998 X Games, San Diego.

Another version of extreme sports takes place behind the scenes, away from the glory that comes with television coverage and cheering crowds. These athletes prefer to play in the woods, alone with nature and the elements. They're the mountain climbers, the backcountry skiers and snowboarders, the explorers. They'll never get a gold medal for what they do, and they probably wouldn't want one anyway. They're doing what they do because they love it, not because it attracts a crowd.

Most people agree that for a sport to be extreme, it has to be difficult, at least for the beginner. It must require specialized skills and techniques. It also requires an adventurous attitude—the kind of attitude that says

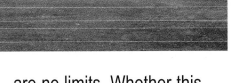

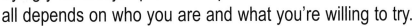

are no limits. Whether this means skating at top speed down a hilly sidewalk or just trying your first jump on a ramp all depends on who you are and what you're willing to try.

Extreme sports can be dangerous, but being extreme doesn't mean being foolish or taking unnecessary risks. No skater wants to risk an injury that might mean never skating again. You can be extreme and still follow safety rules.

If you think you want to be extreme but you're not sure where to start, try aggressive in-line skating. You'll find an adventure with every turn. With in-line skating, you can be as extreme as you want to be.

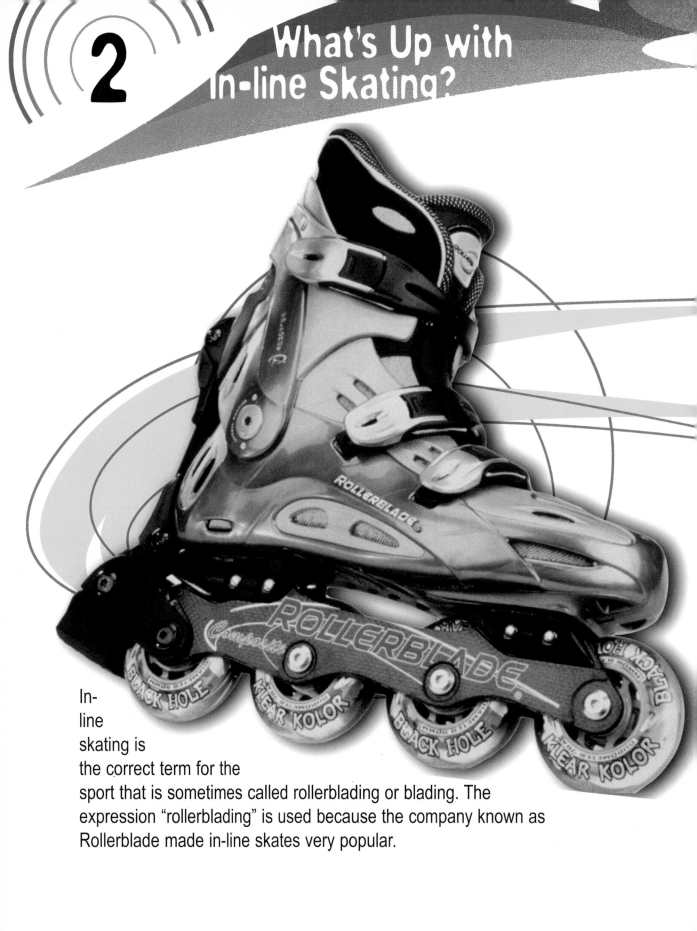

In-line skating is the correct term for the sport that is sometimes called rollerblading or blading. The expression "rollerblading" is used because the company known as Rollerblade made in-line skates very popular.

Clockwise from left: the French Petitbed, 1819; an 1860 in-line skate of unknown manufacture; a 1930s clamp-on in-line skate from the Best-Ever Built Skate Company

It's Nothing New

In-line skates are skates (or "sk8s," if you prefer) that have all four wheels in one straight line. This makes them more like ice skates than traditional roller skates, which have two pairs of side-by-side wheels. People have been roller-skating for hundreds of years. The first pair of in-line skates had wooden wheels. They were common in the Netherlands, a country where many people skate, but were not well-known in the United States.

Until recently, no one had been able to design a roller skate that allowed the user to go as fast or have as much control as ice skaters do. That changed in 1980, when two brothers named Scott and Brennan Olson were digging through a pile of old equipment in a sporting goods store. They found an old in-line skate and they got a great idea. They wanted to redesign the skate to make it faster and easier to use so that they could play ice hockey even when there wasn't any ice. They made a new skate, using a hockey boot, different types of wheels, and

scott olson

a rubber heel brake. Soon they began selling skates out of their home in Minneapolis, Minnesota. This was the beginning of the Rollerblade company.

Rollerblades are not the only in-line skates you can buy, but they're probably the best known. As in-line skating continues to grow in popularity, more sporting goods companies will make more types of in-line skates.

Today's Skaters

At first, in-line skating was seen as a sport for young people and daredevils only. But it didn't take long before people of all ages and abilities wanted to try in-line skating. People enjoy it because it is relatively easy to learn and provides a good workout.

Since the early 1980s, in-line skating has become the most popular new sport among Americans between the ages of twelve and twenty-four. It is also said to be the fastest growing sport in the world.

Different Skates for Different Folks

People in-line skate in many different ways and for different reasons. Some people skate for relaxation, some for exercise. Many people play roller-hockey while wearing in-line skates. Other people skate freestyle, which is like dancing on in-line skates (similar to figure skating on ice). And some people skate to be extreme. The main types of skating are:

Recreational— skating just for fun. Recreational skaters skate in a park or around their neighborhood, after school and on weekends. They skate to relax, be outdoors and enjoy themselves.

Fitness—skating to strengthen muscles and build a healthier heart and lungs. Fitness skaters skate for a certain length of time and for a specific number of times each week (for example, thirty minutes, three times per week). They may also skate faster or uphill or do aerobics on skates. Fitness skating overlaps with recreational skating because recreational skaters also get stronger and healthier from skating.

 Cross-training—skating to strengthen skills for other sports. In-line skating is used to cross-train for skiing, bicycling, and running, among other sports.

Roller hockey—playing hockey on in-line skates.

Race or speed skating—skating competitively for speed. Downhill skating, a relatively new type of skating, also involves high-speed skating.

Freestyle—similar to figure skating or ice dancing. Freestyle skaters perform routines set to music.

Aggressive—the extreme version of in-line skating. Aggressive skaters jump, turn in midair, and do grinds, royals, and other stunts on and off rails, ramps, walls, and other obstacles.

People invent new in-line skating sports all the time. Roller Jam, one of the newest, is a rough sport that combines skating with moves from hockey and wrestling. In Roller Jam, teams of skaters skate very fast in a rink with steeply sloped sides. Each team tries to complete a certain number of laps before the other team does.

3 Getting Aggressive

The extreme version of in-line skating is called aggressive skating. Aggressive skating demands excellent basic skating skills, plus the right equipment and lots of practice. To be an aggressive skater, you need precise footwork, great balance, strength, and endurance. And one more thing is crucial: fearlessness.

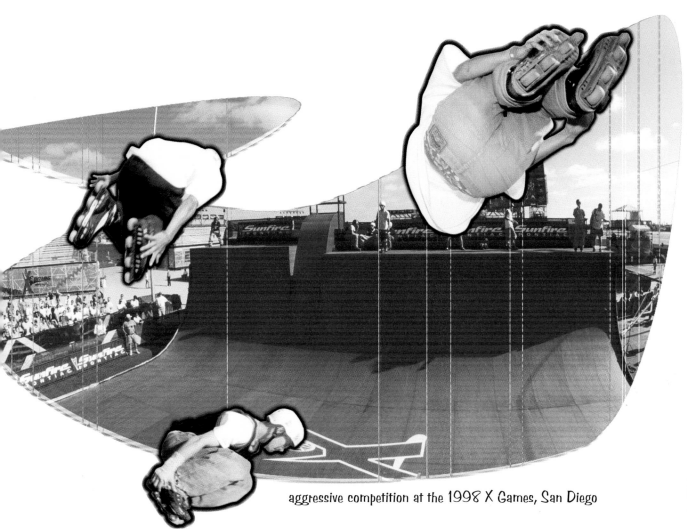

aggressive competition at the 1998 X Games, San Diego

X Sk8

There are two styles of aggressive skating: "street" and "vert." Street-style skating was developed by skaters who lived in the city and used the world around them as their playground. They would skate on curbs, steps, railings, benches, and other objects like an obstacle course.

Street skating can be dangerous not only to skaters themselves but also to passersby. That is why skating in the street or other public places is illegal in many towns and cities. Fortunately, there are skate parks that have benches, steps, and railings for street-style skating, as well as pipes or other ramps for vert-style skating. If you want to try street skating, learn

15

about the laws where you live. Make sure you don't destroy property or injure other people.

Vert skating gets its name from vertical (up and down) ramps—usually empty

Skater Bio

Jenny Curry, of San Luis Obispo, California, was only thirteen when she won the National In-Line Skate Series (NISS) Women's Street Championship in 1997. The following year, she won the street competition at the X Games—and those are only two of her many titles. In addition to skating, Jenny likes to play basketball.

swimming pools or walls—that skaters use to do stunts. For the aggressive in-line skater, there is no bigger rush than vert skating. It is extremely fast and seems to defy gravity. Like most sports, it can also be dangerous. Only experienced skaters with the proper safety equipment should try vert skating.

ASA competition, Philadelphia

The ASA: An Aggressive Organization

Some aggressive skaters are not content to skate just for fun. They want to compete against other skaters and show the world their best and most extreme tricks. Most aggressive-skating competition is governed by the Aggressive Skaters Association (ASA). The ASA produces the skating shows on ESPN and ESPN2 and also oversees the MTV Sports and Music Festival, which includes an aggressive skating competition. The ASA produces both professional and amateur skating events. Professional skaters earn money by skating in competitions just like other professional athletes.

In 1998, the ASA Pro Tour World Championships and the ASA North American Amateur Championships were held in Las Vegas. More than 40,000 people came to see the best aggressive in-line skaters in the world. Athletes from twenty-one countries competed over a four-day period. As aggressive skating grows in popularity, you can expect to see more competitions like these.

Like all good athletes, experienced skaters make aggressive skating look easy. They jump and twist and fly over halfpipes, usually landing safely on their blades. But aggressive skating—like any sport—is risky. You can get hurt. Using the right equipment, including the proper safety gear, can help prevent the most serious injuries.

Without safety equipment, injuries from aggressive skating would be very serious. A minor fall could easily cause permanent damage, like a brain injury or paralysis. All good aggressive skaters wear safety gear.

Jenny Curry at the 1998 X Games, San Diego

If you're thinking, "I won't fall," think again. If you want to learn to skate aggressively, you will fall. It's guaranteed. The next time you watch the X Games, remember: every one of the skaters you see has fallen many, many times. And every single one of them wears a helmet.

Skater Bio

Twenty-year-old Matt Salerno from Sydney, Australia, is a top aggressive skater who wins almost every vert competition he enters. There are only two that he didn't win in 1998: the X Games and the asa Championships. In those competitions, Matt came in second. His best friend, Cesar Mora, was the winner.

Sk8 with Your Head-
Not on It

The most important piece of skating safety equipment is your helmet. A helmet can mean the difference between a minor fall and serious, permanent brain damage—or death.

An injury to the head is the most serious thing that can happen to an athlete (or to anybody, for that matter). Your skull alone cannot protect your brain from the impact of a fall, especially if you fall from a height or

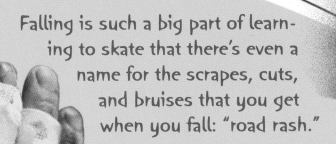

Falling is such a big part of learning to skate that there's even a name for the scrapes, cuts, and bruises that you get when you fall: "road rash."

onto concrete. Any experienced skater will tell you: skating without a helmet is just plain stupid. This is true no matter how long you have been skating or how experienced you have become.

You can buy a helmet at any bicycle or skating shop. Your helmet should fit well, and it should have a sticker inside that states that it has been approved by one of the product safety organizations that rate helmets. (Snell and ANSI/ASTM are the names you will see most often on these stickers.) If you fall and dent your helmet, *get a new one*. Only a helmet in good condition will protect your brain—and you can't get a new one of those.

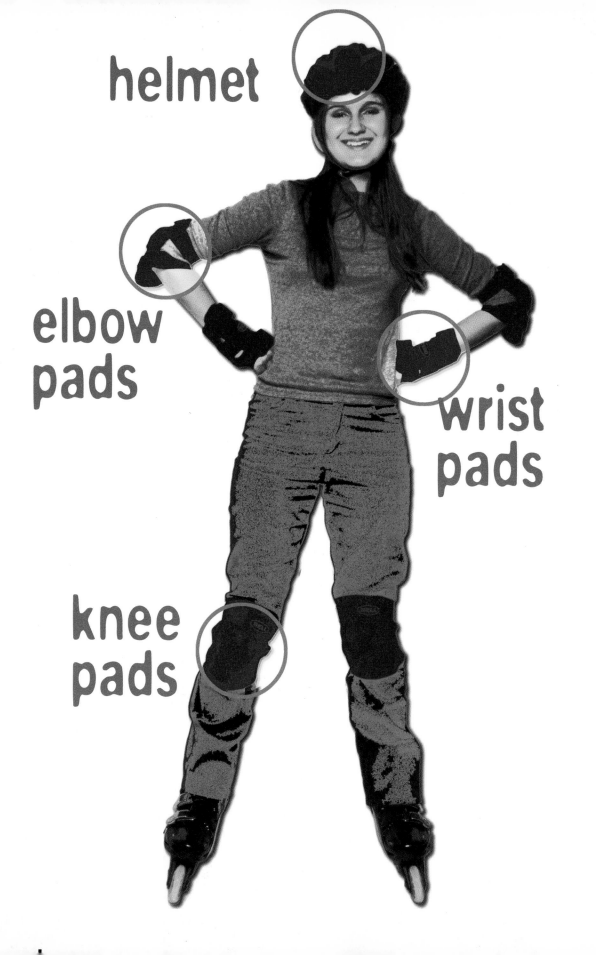

helmet

elbow
pads

wrist
pads

knee
pads

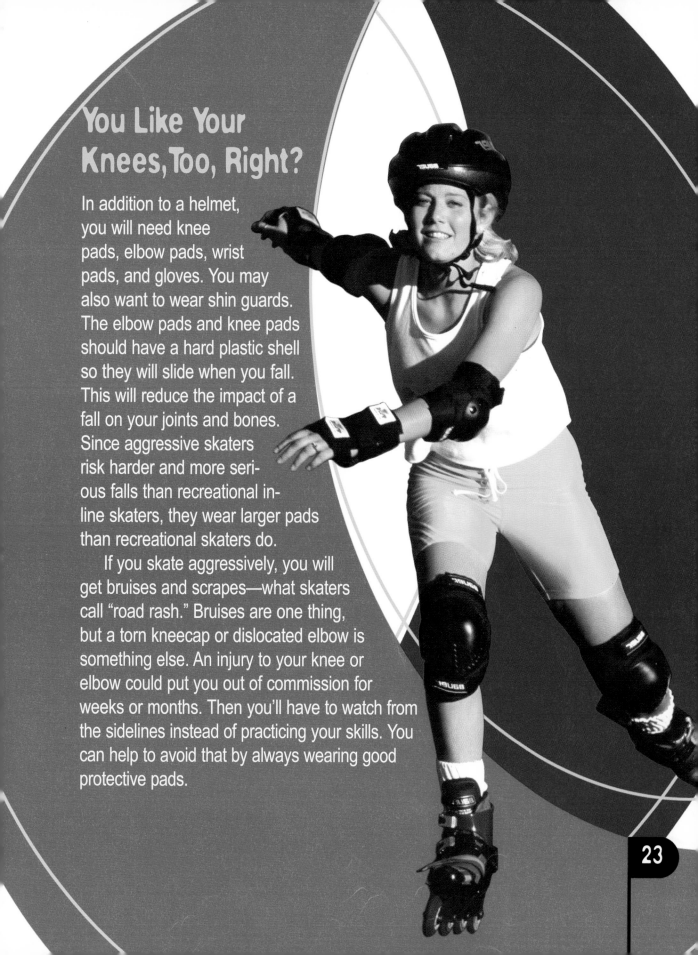

You Like Your Knees, Too, Right?

In addition to a helmet, you will need knee pads, elbow pads, wrist pads, and gloves. You may also want to wear shin guards. The elbow pads and knee pads should have a hard plastic shell so they will slide when you fall. This will reduce the impact of a fall on your joints and bones. Since aggressive skaters risk harder and more serious falls than recreational in-line skaters, they wear larger pads than recreational skaters do.

If you skate aggressively, you will get bruises and scrapes—what skaters call "road rash." Bruises are one thing, but a torn kneecap or dislocated elbow is something else. An injury to your knee or elbow could put you out of commission for weeks or months. Then you'll have to watch from the sidelines instead of practicing your skills. You can help to avoid that by always wearing good protective pads.

23

It's pretty obvious that if you want to skate you are going to need skates. You will want to buy your skating equipment from a skate shop. (Most skate shops also sell skateboards, snowboards and equipment for other extreme sports.) The products in a skate shop may be more expensive than those sold in a large sporting goods store, but they will usually be of higher quality. Also, the people who work in skate shops understand the equipment. They can answer your questions and help you find what you need.

Is This Skate Aggressive Enough?

Different styles of in-line skating require different types of skates. Aggressive skaters want to be as close to the ground as possible for maximum control and balance, so skates for aggressive skating are built low, with very small wheels. The wheels are also very hard, so that they can go over rough surfaces and survive hard landings without wearing out.

Bearings and Rockers

Good in-line skates have something called bearings. Bearings are small steel balls that

aggressive
skates

allow wheels to spin smoothly. Each wheel has two sets of bearings. There are many different types of bearings, and better skates have better bearings. This means that the skates will cost more, but they will also perform better and last longer. Most aggressive skaters look for bearings that will work even at high speeds.

Another word you'll hear a lot around the skate park is "rockering." When skates are rockered, the wheels do not all lie flat on the ground at the same time. For example, on a rockered four-wheel skate, the center wheels are set a little taller than the front and back wheels. So on a flat surface, the front and back wheels are about one-eighth of an inch off the ground. Rockering allows a skater to turn and spin faster. It also causes the skate to be less stable and harder to control at higher speeds.

Before you try rockering your skates, make sure that you are comfortable skating on flat skates with all the wheels on the ground. When you're ready, a more experienced skater or the staff at the skate shop can show you how to rocker your skates.

Rate That Skate

Skate bearings have ratings like ABEC-1 and ABEC-3. That means they have been rated by the Annular Bearing Engineer Council (ABEC), a group that assesses bearings for quality. Some skaters claim that skates with an ABEC-5 rating are the fastest, but other skaters say that there is no evidence that this is true.

Many aggressive skaters prefer a short wheel base. The wheel base is the length of all the wheels combined, from front to back. The longer the wheel base, the faster and more stable the skate. A shorter wheel base is less stable, but allows the skater more control for turning and spinning. Speed skaters use a very long wheel base. Aggressive skaters use a shorter wheel base. The difference between a long and short wheel base may be only a fraction of an inch, but it makes a big difference in how the skate performs.

How to Rock

Aggressive skaters often modify their skates by rockering them. The small parts on skates that go between the wheels and the runners are called frame spacers. Many skates have oval-shaped frame spacers that can be flipped over to rocker the skates. Some skate shops sell "hop-up" kits, which include frame spacers, bearing spacers, and axles, and are used for rockering as well as repairing skates.

In general, aggressive skates:

 Are built low to the ground.

 Have four wheels. (Racing skates have five.)

 Have accessories like grind plates that let a skater "grind" on curbs and slide on rails without damaging the skate's frame.

 Have smaller wheels than recreational skates—smaller wheels are easier to maneuver.

racing skates

There's one other thing that you should know about aggressive in-line skates: they don't have brakes. (So make sure you learn how to stop!)

In-line skates should fit snugly, though they should have a little extra "wiggle room" at the toes. Unlike with hiking or running shoes, your toes should touch the front of the boot—but they shouldn't be jammed in.

The best-known brand of in-line skate is Rollerblade, which were the first skates that were widely available in North America. Other good skate makers are Ultra Wheels, Bauer, Roces, Salomon, and K2. The salesperson in a skate shop will ask you about your experience and your skating goals. With that information, he or she can recommend a brand and model of skate that is right for you. Take your time before you buy. Go to more than one shop, get different opinions, and speak to other skaters before you make a decision.

After you buy your skates, you'll need to maintain them by keeping them in good condition. It's important to know some basic maintenance and repair techniques so that your skates will last a long time and give you top performance. People in the skate shop and other skaters can teach you how to do this.

Ouch! Is There a Helmet for My Wallet?

Quality skates are definitely pricey. If you really want to skate with the safest and best equipment, you won't be able to get away that cheaply. But once you own skates and safety equipment, you're all set—there's nothing else you will need. Here are some ways to save a few bucks:

Try Before You Buy

You can rent skates before you buy them. This will give you time to make sure that you like the sport and the skate model you've chosen before investing a lot of money. Most skate shops rent skates. If after renting you decide to buy skates, the skate shop might deduct your rental fee from the sale price.

BOARD AND SKATE

Sale 30% Off
Snowboards
Boots
Bindings

Sale 30% Off
Snowboards
Boots
Bindings

ROLLERBLA

RENT THE
EXPERIENCE

'Tis the Season . . .

When you shop can save you money. The in-line "season" begins around the end of March. Many skate shops reduce their prices in January and February to sell old merchandise and make room for new models. You can often find last year's styles at a huge discount.

Skates with a History

You also might want to buy a pair of used skates. Someone who wears the same size as you may have upgraded to better equipment or lost interest in the sport. Look for signs and ads around skate shops and where kids skate. If you don't see anyone selling a pair in your size, consider putting up your own ad saying that you want to buy a pair of used skates. Also check used sporting goods stores if there are any near where you live.

Most skaters agree that used skates in good condition and made by a reputable company (like any of the brands previously mentioned) are better than cheap or "off-brand" new skates (like the kind you would find in a discount store). They'll last longer and give you better performance.

Remember: Don't skimp on protection! Used skates and knee pads in good condition are fine, but your helmet must be new.

Basic in-line skating isn't hard to learn, but aggressive skating is not easy. The guys and girls you see at the X Games have practiced for many hours over many weeks and months. And they're still practicing. If they stopped practicing, they wouldn't be good anymore.

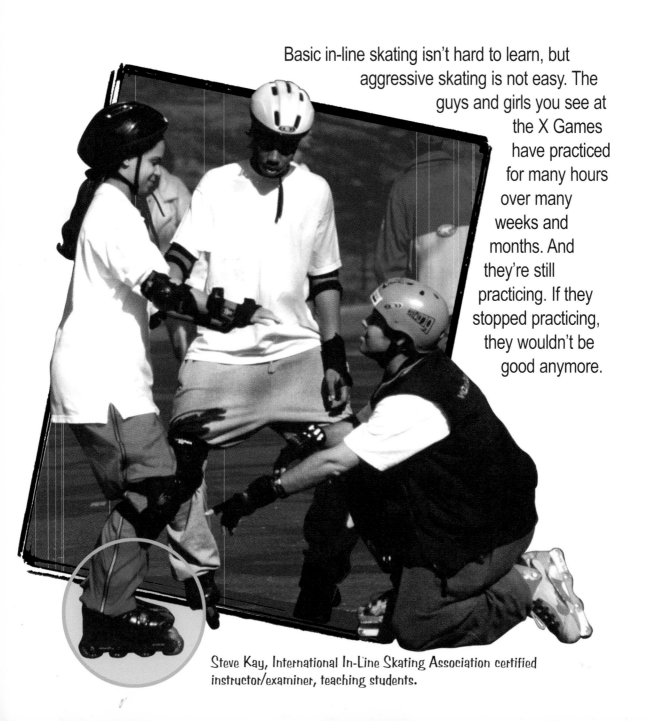

Steve Kay, International In-Line Skating Association certified instructor/examiner, teaching students.

You've Got to Know the Alphabet Before You Can Learn to Read

You can't launch off a halfpipe or grind down a railing before you know how to skate down the sidewalk! Before you try aggressive skating, you have to master the basics. Make sure you are comfortable with:

 Skating forward.

 Skating backward, or "fakie."

 backward swizzle

a-frame turn

Turning.

 Stopping. You should know how to do either a T-stop (by putting one skate behind you and pressing down while also pressing down the wheel edge of your other skate) or a V-stop (by turning your toes inward or your heels outward until your skates touch each other).

t-stop

Freestyle skater Steve Kay guides a student through a T-stop in New York City's Central Park.

Don't underestimate how difficult aggressive skating can be. Besides knowing the basics, you should:

 Know how to control the inside and outside edges of your skates.

Be able to skate with your feet parallel and your knees bent.

 Be strong enough to hold yourself in a tucked position.

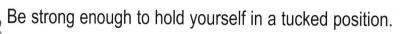 Own full protective gear including elbow guards, knee guards, wrist guards, and a regulation bicycle helmet.

tucked "a" position

Next, Read a Book for Beginners . . .

If you are already a good skater and aggressive skating looks like fun to you, there are certain moves you should practice. These are the basic building blocks that aggressive skating moves are built from:

single-foot glide

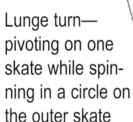

- Lunge turn— pivoting on one skate while spinning in a circle on the outer skate

- T-stop

- Single-foot glide

- 180-degree transition—changing from forward to backward or backward to forward in mid-roll

As you get better, you'll still want to practice skating uphill and downhill and jumping on and off curbs while still skating.

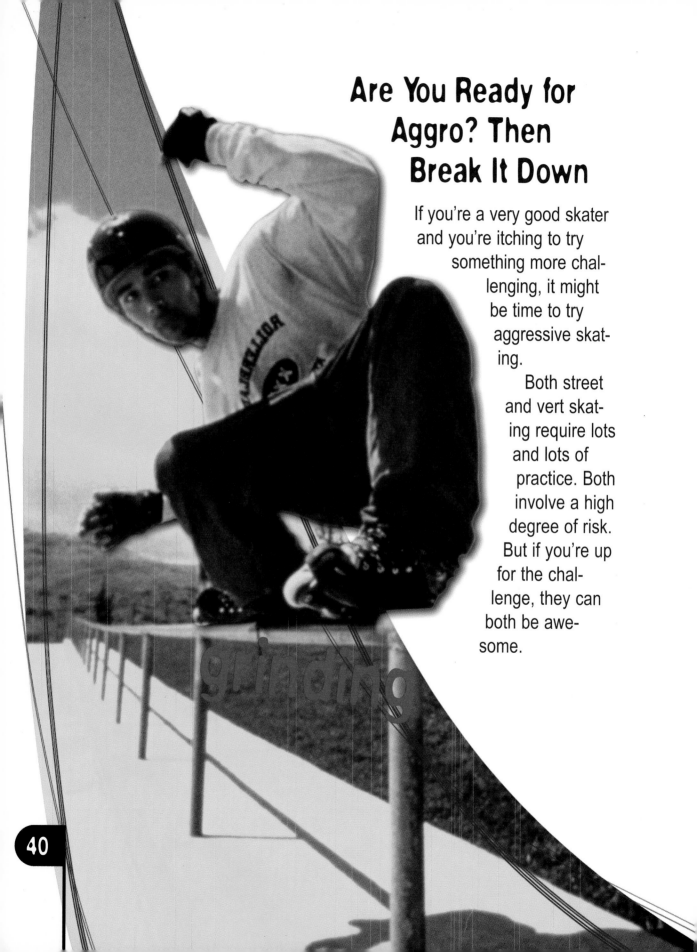

Are You Ready for Aggro? Then Break It Down

If you're a very good skater and you're itching to try something more challenging, it might be time to try aggressive skating.

Both street and vert skating require lots and lots of practice. Both involve a high degree of risk. But if you're up for the challenge, they can both be awesome.

Basic Street Moves

There are a zillion different street moves, and once you get good at several you will probably want to make up your own. These are the basic moves that every aggressive skater should know:

Grinding

Grinding is the most basic aggressive skating move. In a grind, a skater jumps from a regular skating surface onto the edge of a cement block or railing and slides or grinds across the surface. Then the skater jumps off the railing, lands back on the original surface, and continues skating.

Grinding is done with the frame of the skate (the place where the wheels are attached to the boot). As you can probably guess, grinding is pretty hard on skates. That is why skates designed for aggressive skating have grind plates to keep the skate from breaking or wearing out from grinding.

Grinding may look easy but it is tough to learn! Expect to fall a lot while learning how to grind—and make sure you are wearing your safety gear.

Stair Riding

Stair riding, or skating up and down steps, is like doing many curb-jumps in a row. Try it first on wide or deep (not steep) steps, and don't try more than four or five steps at first. As you get better, you can increase the number of steps and the steepness of the stairs. There are some stairs that are just too steep for riding, though—be smart and stay away from those.

Other basic street moves include jumping (onto or over objects), curb jumping, and hill riding.

Basic Vert Moves

Vert skating requires lots of time and practice. You should only attempt it after you are very comfortable and confident on skates.

If and when you are ready to try vert skating, you will need top-quality

safety gear, because you will fall. When you feel yourself start to fall, try to tuck your skates under your rear and slide on your plastic-covered knee pads. In other words, try to get some plastic between you and the cement. Also, learn vert skating on a good ramp, one that is wide and has a big flat area below it.

The Transition

When you first try vert skating, don't expect to do aerial stunts right away! First you must master the transition. The transition is the lower part of the wall—the part that curves up but is not completely vertical. It is the transition between the horizontal and vertical skating surfaces.

Watch other skaters. You'll see that only the most advanced skaters skate straight into the ramp and up the wall. Everyone else carves turns in the transition. Even the most advanced skaters started out this way.

After you become confident skating up and down the transition, try a basic trick such as a small jump into a turn at the top of the arc. At first you will be able to jump only one or two inches. If you can eventually complete a full turn, you should be very proud! Keep practicing and soon you will be able to jump higher and catch more air.

Katie Brown,
1998 X Games,
San Diego

Break It Down

No one was born knowing how to skate aggressively. Even today's best skaters had to start at the beginning. Serious aggressive skaters respect the difficulty of the sport. They don't try to bluff their way through.

Skater Bio

Fabiola DaSilva dominates competitive vert skating. Fabiola, a nineteen-year-old from Brazil, won every competition in 1998 except the ASA Championships. (Japan's Ayumi Kawasaki won there.) Her talents are not confined to vert skating, though. On the ASA World Pro Tour, Fabiola was the overall tour champion in both street and vert.

They know that even the simplest trick requires control, skill, and practice—lots of practice.

Difficult stunts and tricks are easier to learn if you think of them as a string of smaller, less complicated moves performed one after the next.

First, carefully observe skaters doing the stunt properly. Ask them questions:

What's the first thing I need to know about this stunt? What's the hardest thing about it? How should I begin? This will help you break down the stunt into separate components. Components are pieces that are put together to form a whole.

Learn the first component by itself. Practice just that piece of the stunt. Then add the next component. Now you have a new, slightly longer component. Practice that sequence until you are comfortable with it. When that longer sequence of moves becomes easier and more natural, add a third component—and practice all three together. When that new sequence of moves is easier, add a fourth. Keep adding new components in this way, until you can execute the whole stunt.

Always New Tricks to Learn

Very advanced aggressive skaters have learned hundreds of stunts, and they also invent their own moves. Mastering every new stunt requires hard work and practice—breaking the stunt into smaller moves, practicing each separately, then putting it all together.

Practice, watch other skaters, ask questions, and be persistent. Once you know the basics, the possibilities are endless!

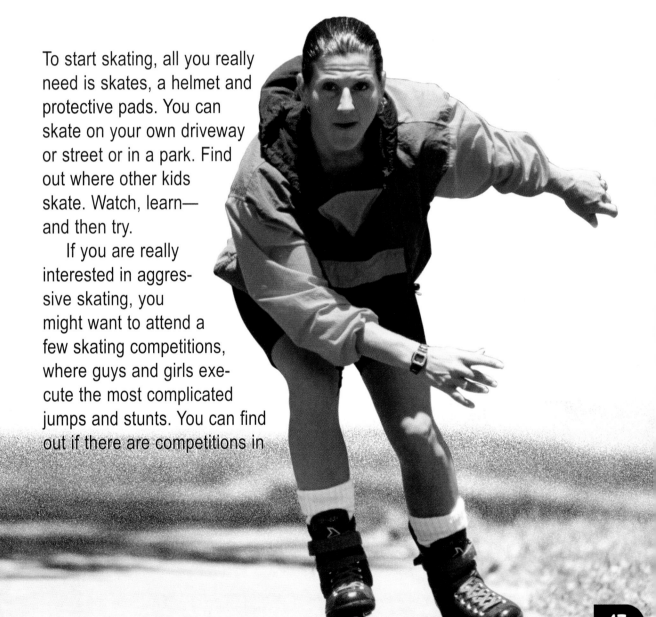

To start skating, all you really need is skates, a helmet and protective pads. You can skate on your own driveway or street or in a park. Find out where other kids skate. Watch, learn— and then try.

If you are really interested in aggressive skating, you might want to attend a few skating competitions, where guys and girls execute the most complicated jumps and stunts. You can find out if there are competitions in

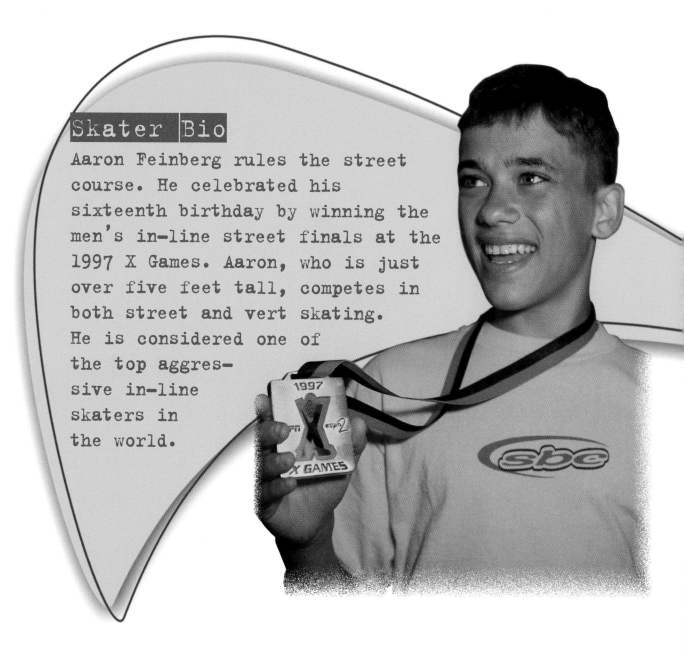

Skater Bio

Aaron Feinberg rules the street course. He celebrated his sixteenth birthday by winning the men's in-line street finals at the 1997 X Games. Aaron, who is just over five feet tall, competes in both street and vert skating. He is considered one of the top aggressive in-line skaters in the world.

your area by asking other skaters. Many skating Web sites also list local and regional competitions.

The Aggressive Skaters Association puts out a schedule listing all official competitions that the association sanctions. Just as in other sports, the winners of local competitions compete in regional games, and the winners of the regional games compete in national games. The world's best aggressive

skaters compete in the ASA World Championships and the X Games.

After you have been skating for a while, you may want to enter a competition to see how your skills match up against the skills of other kids. Lots of people enjoy their sport more when they compete against others and perform in front of people.

Aaron Feinberg at the 1998 X Games, San Diego

Young spectators at the 1997 X Games, San Diego

One way to decide if you are the competitive type is to set up some fun races or contests with friends who skate. That will give you a good sense of whether you flourish or freeze up when matched against other skaters. Even if you don't think competition is for you, you might enjoy watching other skaters compete. Going to an amateur or pro competition is also a great way to find out about the latest tricks and hottest gear.

Whether you prefer to show your skills to the whole world or keep them in the local skate park, aggressive in-line skating is a great sport for anyone who enjoys a fast, thrilling ride. Practice hard, stay safe, and have fun!

Top Ten Places to Skate

These areas were named as the best places to skate in the United States by people who participated in a survey conducted by Rollerblade.

Boulder Creek Path, Boulder, CO

Central Park, New York, NY

Fairmount Park, Philadelphia, PA

Fort Lauderdale Beach, Fort Lauderdale, FL

Golden Gate Park, San Francisco, CA

Lakefront Path, Chicago, IL

The Lakes (Isles/Calhoun/Cedar/Harriet),
       Minneapolis, MN

Rock Creek Park, Washington, DC

The Strand, Pacific Palisades, CA

Veloway at Circle C, Austin, TX

X-Planations

air Having both skates entirely off the ground.

antirocker A wheel configuration used by many railsliders. The larger wheels are at the toe and heel and the smaller wheels in the middle.

bashing Another word for stair riding. Also called stair bumping and stair bashing.

bearings The metal balls inside the wheels of a skate. There are two sets of bearings in each wheel.

bearing spacers Small plastic or metal parts that fit in between a skate's bearings so that the axles can go through the wheels.

carve To skate in a long, curving arc.

coping A bar or rounded section at the top of a ramp.

drop in To enter a ramp from the top.

fakie To skate backwards. Also used as a prefix for any trick done backwards, as in a "fakie-360."

frame The part of a skate that attaches the wheels to the base.

frame spacers The part of a skate between the wheels and the runners.

grind To skate with the edge of the frame against a curb or other obstacle.

grind plates Flat metal or hard plastic plates that are bolted to the skate's runners for grinding and sliding. Protects the skates from wearing down.

halfpipe A U-shaped ramp used in vert skating.

hop-up kits Kits that include frame spacers, bearing spacers, and axles, used for upgrading or repairing skates.

rail slides A trick in which the skater slides along a rail.

road rash Scrapes, cuts, and other injuries suffered when a skater falls or slides on a hard surface such as pavement or concrete.

rockering To arrange the skate wheels at different heights to make the skate more like an ice skate with a curved blade. This is usually done by flipping the frame spacers, which raises the front and rear wheels slightly. Rockering makes the skate less stable but allows the skater to turn and spin faster.

skitching Hanging on to some moving vehicle and letting it pull you along—dangerous, illegal, and stupid. Term comes from "skate hitching."

stair riding A stunt where the skater rides down a set of steps. Bumpy, but with a good stance and balance, it is fun. Always use protective gear when trying stair riding!

street Refers to the style of aggressive skating that uses everyday objects like stairs, curbs, and benches to do stunts.

transition The curve of a ramp between the flat area and the vertical section.

vert Short for "vertical," meaning up and down. Refers to the style of aggressive skating that uses vertical walls to do stunts.

wheel rotation A way to extend the life of a skate's wheels by periodically switching the wheels—for example, moving the front wheels to the back and the back ones to the front.

Extreme Info

Aggressive Skaters Association (ASA)
13468 Beach Avenue
Marina del Rey, CA 90292
Phone: (310) 823-1865
Fax: (310) 823-4146
e-mail: asa@aggroskate.com
Web site: http://www.aggroskate.com

Canadian In-Line & Roller Skating Association (CIRSA)
679 Queens Quay West, Unit 117
Toronto, ON M5V 3A9
Canada
Phone: (800) 958-000 (in Canada) or (416) 260-5959 (outside Canada)
Fax: (416) 260-0798
e-mail: cirsa@ican.net
Web site: http://www.home.ican.net/~cirsa

International In-Line Skating Association (IISA)
372 Farragut Avenue, Suite 400
Kensington, MD 20895
Phone: (301) 942-9770
Fax: (301) 942-9771
Web site: http://www.iisa.org
Provides information about in-line skating in general (not just aggressive skating).

Web Sites

Skating is all over the Web—there are hundreds of Web sites about aggressive skating and other extreme sports. Most contain links to other skating sites. Lots of aggressive skaters have their own individual Web sites too. If you have a Web site, you may want to include information on aggressive skating and link it to other skating sites. Here are some of the biggest and best sites:

Aggressive Skaters Association (ASA)
http://www.aggroskate.com

The All In-Line Skating Web Site
http://www.home.clara.net/solomons/inlinesk8

Blade GIRLZ
http://www.hotrails.com/bladegrl.htm

Hot Rails
http://www.hotrails.com

InLine America
http://www.whywalk.com

Inline Online
http://bird.taponline.com:80/inline

N2inline.com, the Inline Skaters Web site
http://n2inline.com

Skate FAQs (answers to many skating questions)
http://www.skatefaq.com

Skating the Infobahn
http://www.skatecity.com

Women's Aggressive Skating Network
http://www.xtremecentral.com/WASN/WASNintro.htm

Zines and Mags

There are dozens of magazines and zines devoted to aggressive skating. Many of them also cover skateboarding, snowboarding, and music. The following are some of the best known:

Box
1223 Wilshire Blvd., #893
Santa Monica, CA 90403
(351) 451-8061

Daily Bread
P.O. Box 82146
San Diego, CA 92138
Phone: (619) 270-6656
Fax: (619) 270-4256
Web site: http://www.dbmag.com

Sequence
P.O. Box 720635
San Jose, CA 95172
Web site: http://www.sequencemag.com

Skater
660 Venice Boulevard, Suite 165
Venice, CA 90291
Phone: (310) 827-5242
Fax: (310) 827-5597
e-mail: skatermag@aol.com

Skating.com: The Skater's Online Magazine
Shafran Interactive Media
P.O. Box 5097
Hoboken, NJ 07030
Web site: http://www.skating.com

X Sk8
P.O. Box 65171
Washington, DC 20035-5171
Phone: (202) 362-6159
Fax: (202) 686-5717

Many of the Web sites listed in Extreme Info can give you a list of skate parks in your area. If there is no skate park near where you live, consider starting one! *Skating.com, The Skater's Online Magazine,* offers tips on starting a skate park.

In-line Skate Camps

If you live and breathe aggressive skating and want to improve your skills, a skate camp might be the place for you. Here are a few to consider:

Camp Santa Rosa
c/o Snoopy's Gallery
1665 West Steele Lane
Santa Rosa, CA 95403
Phone: (800) 959-3385
Fax: (707) 546-0391

Greg Keim's American In-line Skating
4255 Hunt Club Circle, Suite 1412
Fairfax, VA 22033
Phone: (703) 277-2628
Fax: (703) 277-2629
e-mail: keim@his.com
Web site: http://www.his.com/americaninline

Tahoe Extreme Sports Camps
(800) PRO-CAMP (776-2267)
Web site: http://www.800procamp.com/extremecamp.html

The Woodward Camp
Box 93, Route 45
Woodward, PA 16882
Phone: (814) 349-5633
Fax: (814) 349-5643
e-mail: office@woodward.com
Web site: http://www.woodwardcamp.com/ xcamp.htm

For a list of certified instructors in your area, contact the IISA.

Competition

Here are the major events sponsored by the Aggressive Skating Association (ASA):

ASA Pro Tour
ASA World Championships
ESPN X Games
MTV Sports & Music Fest
Ultimate Inline Challenge

The ASA also sponsors an amateur competition circuit with events all over the country. The amateur circuit ends with the Amateur Championships, which take place at the ASA World Championships in October.

You can check the event listings at the Web sites listed in Extreme Info for information about the many other aggressive skating events throughout the year. For information about the Panasonic National In-Line Skate Series (NISS), contact:

NISS
3101 Washington Boulevard
Marina del Rey, CA 90292
(310) 823-1826
Web site: http://www.agrosk8.com

Extreme Reading

Chalmers, Aldie. *The Fantastic Book of In-Line Skating.* Brookfield, CT: Millbrook Press, 1997.

Dugard, Martin. *In-Line Skating Made Easy: A Manual for Beginners with Tips for the Experienced.* Old Saybrook, CT: Globe Pequot Press, 1996.

Edwards, Chris. *The Young Inline Skater.* New York: DK Publishing, 1996.

Feineman, Neil, with Team Rollerblade. *Wheel Excitement.* New York: William Morrow & Co., 1998.

Gorman, S. S. *Daredevil Bladers.* New York: Pocket Books, 1996.

Millar, Cam. *In-Line Skating Basics.* New York: Sterling Publishing Co., 1996.

Miller, Liz. *Get Rolling: The Beginner's Guide to In-Line Skating.* New York: McGraw-Hill, 1998.

Powell, Mark, and John Svensson. *In-Line Skating.* Champaign, IL: Human Kinetics Publishing, 1997.

Rappelfeld, Joel. *The Complete In-Line Skater.* New York: St. Martin's Press, 1996.

Sullivan, George. *In-Line Skating: A Complete Guide for Beginners.* New York: Dutton Children's Books, 1993.

Index

A

aggressive skates, attributes of, 28–30
  See also *bearings; rockering*
aggressive skating, 13, 14, 15, 17, 18, 19–20,
  23, 25–27, 28, 29, 30, 34, 39, 44, 49
    basic building blocks, 39–40
    practice, how to, 45–46
    teacher of, 25
  See also *competitions; street skating; vert
  skating*
Aggressive Skaters Association (ASA), 17, 48
    ASA Pro Tour World Championships,
17–18, 49
    ASA North American Amateur
Championship, 18
    ASA Championships, 20, 44 amateur
skating, 17
Annular Bearing Engineer Council (ABEC), 27

B

bearings, 25, 27
bearing spacers, 28
blading, 8
brain injury, 19–20

C

competitions, 5, 16, 17, 18, 20, 44, 48–49, 50
cross-training, 12
Curry, Jenny, 16

D

DaSilva, Fabiola, 44

E

extreme skating, 5, 14
extreme sports, 6–7

F

Feinberg, Aaron, 48
fitness skating, 12
frame spacers, 28
freestyle, 13

G

Gengo, Kate, 25
grinding, 41
grind plates, 41

H

halfpipes, 19, 35
helmet, 20–21, 23, 33, 38
    ratings, 21
  See also *brain injury*
"hop-up" kits, 28

I

in-line skates, 8, 9–10
    bearings, 25–27
    brand names, 30
    buying/renting, 24, 30, 33
    fit, 30
    repair/maintenance, 28, 30
    used, 33
  See also *ratings*

K

Kawasaki, Ayumi, 44

L

lunge turn, 39

M

Mora, Cesar, 20

N

National In-Line Skate Series (NISS) Women's
  Street Championship, 16
Netherlands, 9

O

Olson, Scott and Brennan, 9

P

professional skaters, 17
protective pads, 23

R

race or speed skating, 13
ratings
    skate bearings, 27
    helmets, 21
"road rash," 21, 23

rockering, 27–29
Rollerblade, 8, 10, 30
rollerblading, 8
roller hockey, 13
Roller Jam, 13

S

safety gear, 19–20, 23, 41, 42
Salerno, Matt, 20
skates (see *in-line skates*)
skate shops, 24, 29, 30
skating
    basic moves, 35–37
    additional moves, 37–38
  See also *aggressive skating*
stair riding, 41
street skating, 15, 40
    basic moves, 41, 48
    competitions, 44, 48

T

T-stop, 37
transition, vert skating, 42

V

vert skating, 15, 40
    transition, 42, 48
V-stop, 37

W

wheel base, 29
Women's Aggressive Skating Network
  (WASN), 25

X

X Games, 5, 16, 20, 34, 48, 49

Credits

Special Thanks

Thanks to IISA examiner/certified instructor Steve Kay, and his sponsor, Salomon.

About the Author

Laura Kaminker has been a freelance writer for fifteen years. She has written books, magazine articles, and educational videos and has worked with teenagers as a teacher and counselor. She lives in New York City with her partner, Allan Wood, and their two dogs.

Photo Credits

Cover photo Tony Donaldson; pp. 2, 4, 5, 15, 16, 17, 18, 19, 21, 26, 43, 44, 48, 49 © Tony Donaldson; pp. 6–7, 22, 24, 28, 31, 32, 34, 35, 36, 37, 38, 45 by Thaddeus Harden; pp. 8 © Rollerblade, Inc.; p. 9 © National Museum of Roller Skating, Lincoln, Nebraska; p 10 © Sky Fitness, Inc.; pp. 11 © Photri/Microstock; p. 12 © Stephen Dunn/Allsport; pp. 14, 40 © Ken Greer/1998 Rollerblade, Inc.; p. 23 © Karl Weatherly/Mountain Stock; p. 29 © Betsy Porter Joseph/SportsChrome USA; p. 42 © Brian Drake/SportsChrome West Inc.; p. 47 © Robert Tringall/SportsChrome East/West Inc.; p. 50 © Jamie Courie/Allsport. Thanks to the Princeton Ski Shop in Manhattan for allowing us to shoot the photos on pages 24, 28, and 31 in their store. Thanks also to BLADES Board and Skate in Manhattan for allowing us to shoot the photo on page 32.

Series Design

Oliver H. Rosenberg

Layout

Laura Murawski

Consulting Editor

Amy Haugesag